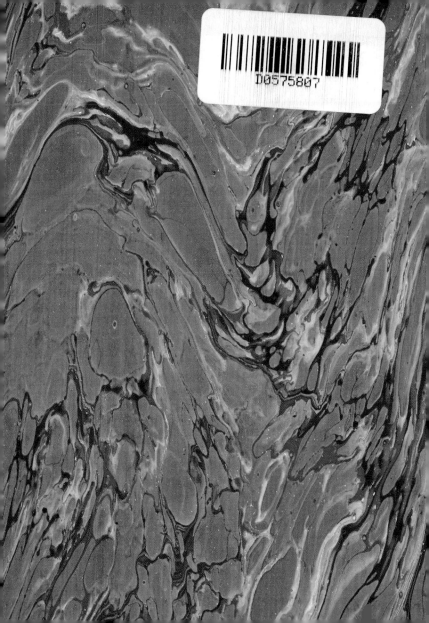

ON THE WINGS OF
ANGELS

ON THE WINGS OF

Angels

EDITED BY PAMELA BLOOM

Ariel Books

Andrews and McMeel
Kansas City

Frontispiece: *Angel*, n.d., Sir Edward Burne-Jones

Title page detail: *Cherubs Floating on a Cloud*, n.d., Spanish School

Book design by Maura Fadden Rosenthal

ISBN: 0-8362-4730-2

ART CREDITS: p. 1: *Resurrection of the Flesh* (detail), n.d., Luca Signorelli; p.6: *Winged Figure*, 1889, Abbott Henderson Thayer; p.9: *The Holy Family in Glory with Saints Francis of Paola and Aloysius Gonzaga* (detail), n.d., Francesco Cappella (called Francesco Daggiu); p.10: *The Ramparts of God's House*, n.d., John Melhuish Strudwick; p. 13: *Nativity* (detail), n.d., Master of Flemalle; p.15: *Annunciation* (detail), n.d., Lorenzo Lotto; pp.16-17: *Mystic Marriage St. Catherine* (detail), n.d., Fra Bartolomeo; p.18: *Olympus: The Fall of the Giants* (detail), n.d., Francisco Bayeu; pp.20-21: *Cupids with a Garland of Flowers*, c.1670, Carlo Maratta; p.22 (inset) *Adoration of the Shepherds* (detail), c.1640, Louis Lenain; pp.22-23: *Triumph of Galatea* (detail), n.d., Raphael; p.24: *Angel*, 1889, Abbott Henderson Thayer; p.27: *Jupiter*, n.d., Gustav Doré; p.28: *Night with Her Train of Stars*, n.d., Edward Robert Hughes; pp.30-31: *The Sacred Grove* (detail), 1884-89, Pierre Puvis de Chavannes; p.32: *Cupid and Psyche* (detail), 1867, Edward Coley Burne-Jones; p.34: *Psyche Loses Sight of Love* (detail), n.d., Matthew Ridley Corbett; p.35: *The Annunciation*, n.d., Gaudenzio; p.36: *The Days of Creation (The First Day)* (detail), n.d., Sir Edward Burne-Jones; p.39: *The Knight of the Holy Grail* (detail), 1912, Frederick Judd Waugh; p.40: *Sistine Madonna* (detail), c. 1513, Raphael.

CONTENTS

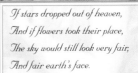

If stars dropped out of heaven,
And if flowers took their place,
The sky would still look very fair,
And fair earth's face.

Winged angels might fly down to us
To pluck the stars,
But we could only long for flowers
Beyond the cloudy bars.

—*Christina Rossetti*

From time immemorial, angels have touched the hearts of all people seeking to penetrate the sacred and the miraculous. From the winged griffins of Mesopotamia to the wrathful archangels of the Bible to the bird totems of Native American shamanism, celestial beings have symbolized humanity's deep longing to glimpse the divine in physical form. A skeptic may seriously argue whether angels exist, but no one can deny that winged wonders have inspired some of the greatest art in the world—from the sculpture of Michelangelo to the poetry of Blake to the oratorios of Haydn.

Who and what *are* angels? There exist as many answers to that question as there are individual souls. But perhaps the secret can be found in the word *angel* itself, which comes from the Greek *angelos* meaning "messenger." Just consider angels to be God's celestial representatives on earth. Whenever God needs a message sent to his beloved children, he sends one of his special messengers. Big or small, winged or not, a tiny spark of light or a great burning bush—divine messengers come in all shapes and sizes.

Everything you would want to know about angels actually

isn't found in the Bible. The best places to discover information about angels are outside the traditional scriptures — in the so called "hidden" books and in the writings of great mystics and poets. Only two angels are called by name in the Bible, and in the early books of the Old Testament they often appear just as ordinary humans dressed in goatskins. It wasn't until the era of the Roman Emperor Constantine in A.D. 312 that angels in Christian art even got halos.

Who believes in angels? In a 1978 Gallup poll, over half the subjects questioned claimed they had some abiding belief in celestial beings. Three out of four teens say they believe in angels. Almost anyone who claims to have encountered an angel says the experience has profoundly changed the way they think about reality. An echo of that blissful moment has stayed with them all of their lives.

How does an ordinary person get to see an angel? The great masters and saints of all religions taught that a sincere prayer from the heart is a good start. Selflessly serving others also seems to magnetize their presence. The yoga sutras of Pantajali, an Indian meditation master, taught how to contact celestial beings by meditating on the light inside one's own head. Whatever your inclination is, we hope this little book on angels and angel lore will give you hints on how to reach the inner chamber of your own angelic self.

Every visible thing in this world is put in the charge of an angel.

THE WORK OF ANGELS

*T*ime after time, angels have appeared to humans incognito, dressed in modern garb and speaking their language. In their most sublime job on earth, angels are deployed to offer comfort, inspiration, and spiritual guidance. Some people also relate stories in which angels have had a tangible impact on the course of human events: disguised as human beings, they may warn someone of impending doom or give advice or guidance that influences the recipient's life in substantial ways.

Angels in the Bible

Some of the patriarchs in the Bible no more expected to meet angels than we do today. Abraham had no idea that the three dusty travelers who appeared one day on his doorstep were actually angels, but at least he had the good heart to immediately offer them bread, milk, and veal. It was only after enjoying Abraham's hospitality that the three angels revealed exactly why they had come—to announce the joyful news that God would grace Sarah with a child, even though she was long past her childbearing years.

Two generations later, Abraham's grandson Jacob was on
his way to fight his brother, Esau, when he met an angel.
Taking him for an adversary, however, Jacob spent the night
wrestling with him. Just before daybreak, when the angel saw
he was not winning, he hit Jacob on the hip, throwing it out
of joint, and pleaded to be released. Jacob finally agreed, on
the condition the stranger first bless him. For that unexpect-
edly soulful request, Jacob was rewarded by God with a new
name—Israel. Later, in a dream, Jacob saw angels walking up
and down a ladder that connected heaven and earth.

None of the desultory citizens of Sodom and Gomorrah
recognized the two angels who visited Lot's house—except Lot
himself. Like his uncle Abraham, Lot served the angels a fine
meal before learning who they were. The next morning, the
angels told Lot and his family to run for their lives from
Sodom and not look back. Lot's wife, who didn't heed the
angelic advice, turned around and dissolved into a pillar of salt.

Angel Advisors

Throughout the ages, both saints and common people
have received guidance from heavenly beings, often in the
form of the "still, small voice" inside. The Greek philosopher
Socrates talked about the "prophetic voice" inside him that

was his constant companion, always opposing him, even in trivial things, if he were ever to take the wrong course. Socrates was tried and condemned for his philosophical views and for corrupting youth. So much did Socrates trust his inner voice that when his angel did not warn him to leave Athens, he decided the death sentence that resulted from his staying was actually a blessing.

Great religions have often been founded on revelations from angels. Muhammad, the founder of the Muslim religion, claimed to have witnessed a beautiful vision of the angel Gabriel, who promised to guide him in his new role of prophet. Muhammad received revelations he believed to be of God, which were written down and became the sacred scripture of Islam, the Koran.

Other religious and political leaders also have felt they have received angelic guidance. Throughout his lifelong quest to unite warring political factions and inspire racial harmony, Abraham Lincoln said he frequently felt the presence of angels about him. Pope Pius XI once confided to the future Pope John XXIII that whenever he had to meet certain people, he would send his guardian angel to talk to them first and smooth the way.

One of the most famous angel advisors of this century belonged to Dorothy Maclean, the founder of Findhorn, a spiritual community in Great Britain. Constantly attuned to her inner voices after ten years of intense meditation, Dorothy was inspired to create gardens whose structure and growth cycles were totally directed by the plant angels, or *devas*, with whom Dorothy conversed. So successful were these beautiful gardens they eventually provided complete sustenance for the entire community, and today visitors speak of the profound sense of peace and joy they experience when viewing the gardens.

Rescue Angels

Angels hover everywhere, ever poised to rescue their human charges from untoward fate, dressed in the costume of each age, humbly dispersing their duties and then joyfully disappearing without even waiting for thanks.

Corrie ten Boom, who became one of the world's great inspirational speakers, felt she received "invisible intervention" when she was released from a German concentration camp because of a clerk's error—just days before all the other women her age were sent to the gas chambers.

Another invisible angel saved the sixteenth-century Italian saint Fillipo Neri, a clergyman and mystic, when he was walking down a very narrow Roman street full of ditches.

As a driverless carriage with four runaway horses came bolting by, Fillipo felt himself lifted up by his hair and taken out of harm's way—without human assistance. Eyewitnesses were left amazed.

St. Francesca Romana was also saved by a guardian angel when she fell into the Tiber River in 1399, but the celestial being was already well known to her. For twenty-four years, this angel had fully appeared to her in the ethereal form of a ten-year-old boy, whose long hair and shining eyes offset the white deaconlike tunic he always wore. In later years, this angel was

replaced by another who always manifested to her in the act of weaving a golden thread. When Francesca was about to die, she watched as this angel spun the golden thread—a symbol of her life—faster and faster until her last breath ran out.

During World War II, after Winston Churchill avoided being killed by a car bomb, he told his wife it was because "something" inside him told him to stop when he approached the car door being held open for him. Instead, he went around to the other side of the car, an act that saved his life when the bomb exploded in his normal seat. Later, he became convinced that inner "something" had been an angelic force.

Many people will be relieved to know that angels even appear in airplane cockpits. Joan Wester Anderson, in her book *Where Angels Walk*, tells the story of two men trying to navigate a small private plane through a solid fog bank over North Carolina. Suddenly they heard a voice on their radio barking out orders instructing them how to land safely. When the pilots went to thank the air-traffic controller, they discovered the airport had lost all radio contact with them and *nobody*— nobody human, that was—had been recorded assisting them. After hearing that startling news, the two pilots never flew a plane again without believing an angel was guiding them.

Inspiring Angels

∞ Many of the great artists of the world have proclaimed their talents to be divine gifts—their inspiration arriving as if on the wings of an angel. Able to write down his compositions in a rambling carriage or in the midst of a noisy café, Mozart claimed that angels sang tunes into his ear. From childhood, the great mystic poet and artist William Blake had visions of spirits and even said angels had taught him to paint. "I am not ashamed to tell you what ought to be told," he once wrote, "that I am under the direction of messages from heaven day and night."

Michelangelo, the sculptor and painter, was more than divinely inspired; he felt himself to be at the service of angels. One day, the story goes, he saw a block of marble he wanted to carve, but the owner refused to sell it to him, saying the marble had no value. Ever attuned to higher forces, however, Michelangelo insisted on buying it, later explaining he had seen imprisoned inside the marble an angel he needed to set free.

Millions of spiritual
creatures walk the Earth
Unseen, both when we wake, and
when we sleep.

—John Milton

ANGEL QUOTES

Be not forgetful to entertain strangers, for thereby some have entertained angels unawares.

—*Hebrews 13:2*

The angels are the dispensers and administrators of the Divine beneficence toward us; they regard our safety, undertake our defense, direct our ways, and exercise a constant solicitude that no evil befall us.

—*John Calvin*

Everywhere, all over the universe animate things are accompanied and guided by masters, because the Father in his infinite wisdom has placed beside every living creature those who can help and sustain them.

—*Yan Su Lu*

Angels at the foot,
And Angels at the head,
And like a curly little lamb
My pretty babe in bed.

—Christina Rossetti

Angels, in the early morning
May be seen the Dews among

—Emily Dickinson

Angels cannot be seen by man with his bodily eyes, but only with the eyes of the spirit which is within him . . .

—Emanuel Swedenborg

It is not known precisely where angels dwell—whether in the air, the void, or the planets. It has not been God's pleasure that we should be informed of their abode.

—Voltaire

Make yourself familiar with the angels, and behold them frequently in spirit; for, without being seen, they are present with you.

—St. Francis de Sales

*The angel ended, and in Adam's ear
So charming left his voice that he awhile
Thought him still speaking, still stood fix'd to hear.*

—John Milton

What's impossible to all humanity may be possible to the metaphysics and physiology of angels.

—Joseph Glanvill

Like angel visits, short and bright.

—John Norris

I have seen a thousand times that angels are human forms, or men, for I have conversed with them as man to man, sometimes with one alone, sometimes with many in company.

—Emanuel Swedenborg

That there are angels and spirits good and bad . . . is so clear from Scripture that no believer, unless he be first of all spoiled by philosophy and vain deceit, can possibly entertain a doubt of it.

—Richard Hurd

The angels were all singing out of tune,
And hoarse with having little else to do,
Excepting to wind up the sun and moon
Or curb a runaway young star or two.

—Lord Byron

I want to be an angel,
And with the angels stand,
A crown upon my forehead,
A harp within my hand.

—Urania Bailey

Visits
Like those of angels, short and far between.

—*Robert Blair*

If some people really see angels where others see only empty space, let them paint the angels; only let not anybody else think they can paint an angel too, on any calculated principles of the angelic.

—*John Ruskin*

We not only live among men, but there are airy hosts, blessed spectators, sympathetic lookers-on, that see and know and appreciate our thoughts and feelings and acts.

—*Henry Ward Beecher*

The more materialistic science becomes, the more angels shall I paint: their wings are my protest in favor of the immortality of the soul.

—*E. C. Burne-Jones*

We should pray to the angels, for
they are given to us as guardians.
—St. Ambrose

WHAT ANGELS LOOK LIKE

*A*ngels come in all shapes and sizes—as various as the humans who see them. In ancient Assyria, divine protectors were thought to look like winged lions, bulls, and eagles, all with human heads. As Christian art developed, angelic beings became more ethereal, depicted with shimmering wings, lithe bodies swathed in white silk, and golden halos around their heads. Fallen angels, like Satan, were usually marked by ugly faces, batlike wings, cloven feet, and serpentine hair. However, to some visionaries wicked angels would appear as irresistibly sensuous, like the lascivious Lilith, the first wife of Adam who later became the bride of the devil.

From the chubby cherubim who, like Cupid, bring gaiety and joy, to the warriorlike archangels who guard the portals of heaven with flaming swords, angels have always appeared in the form in which they could most help their human charges. But sometimes celestial forces have simply manifested themselves as pure light. A middle-aged man reported to H. C. Moolenburgh, a Dutch doctor, that one day at church, he and his fiancée both saw near the altar a brilliant light that almost obliterated the figure of the priest celebrating mass. So intense was the sense of peace and goodwill that descended on them that neither could speak for a while. Afterward, they summoned up the courage to talk to the priest, who claimed he had seen nothing. Still, the experience was so profound that the couple remained convinced it was God's way of blessing their upcoming marriage.

Given the awesome quality of angels, how could common language ever manage to do them justice? From the Bible to the Koran, from the English poet John Donne to the modern novelist Ray Bradbury, some of the world's greatest visionary writers have applied their poetic talents to the challenge of describing God's heavenly hosts. Here are some of the finest examples:

Their faces were living flame; their wings were gold; and for the rest their white was so intense, no snow can match the white they showed. When they climbed down into that flowering Rose, from rank to rank, they shared that peace and ardor which they gained, with wings that fanned their sides.

—Dante

Their garments are white, but with an unearthly whiteness. I cannot describe it, because it cannot be compared to earthly whiteness; it is much softer to the eye. These bright Angels are enveloped in a light so different from ours that by comparison everything else seems dark. When you see a band of fifty, you are lost in amazement. They seem clothed with golden plates, constantly moving, like so many suns.

—Père Lamy

I saw a hundred thousand times a hundred thousand, ten million times ten million, an innumerable and uncountable (multitude) who stand before the glory of the Lord of the Spirits.

—Enoch I

*... The Night of Glory,
more opulent than a thousand moons!
Then angels and revelations waft down
by the grace of their Lord.*

—The Koran, XCVII

The Angel that presided o'er my birth

birth

Said, "Little creature, formed of joy and mirth,

and mirth,

Go love without the help of any thing

on earth."

—William Blake

ON THE THRESHOLD
OF BIRTH AND DEATH

*T*raditionally, angels have stood guard during difficult times of passage in human lives, particularly at birth and at death.

In the Bible, angels often served to herald the birth of great souls, especially when the mother was least expecting it. The birth of Samson, the great warrior with superhuman strength, was announced in this way. The most famous example, however, was the Annunciation—Gabriel's pronouncement to the Virgin Mary of the coming birth of Jesus.

The souls of just-born babies are also said to rest in the hands of angels. According to Jewish lore, when a child is still in its mother's womb, an angel teaches the young soul all it needs to know about truth and mercy. But just as the child is about to take its first breath, another angel taps it on the mouth, causing it to forget everything. For centuries, the ancient rabbis unsuccessfully pondered the rationale behind these peculiar antics, until one day a particularly wise scholar decided that if we remembered everything, we would be in dread of death every day. The scholar believed that God

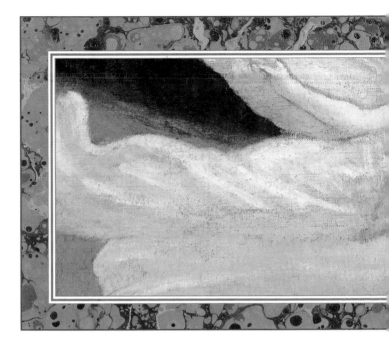

grants us a human existence just so we can relearn what our heart already knows.

No greater comfort can a human being feel than when, on the threshold of life's end, an angel appears to guide one through the stormy straits to heaven. Many people who have had near-death experiences report a shining presence of light that gives them comfort, freedom from pain, and a sense of all-abiding peace. Sometimes assisting angels appear in the

form of loved ones who have already died or even long-lost favorite pets. Tibetan Buddhists meditate their whole lives to be able to recognize the angelic presence of their master as they are dying and before they are reborn into a new body. The great African-American spirituals of former centuries painted a vision of the weary soul being escorted to its heavenly home by celestial beings.

Around our pillows golden ladders rise,
And up and down the skies,
With winged sandals shod,
The angels come, and go, the Messengers of
God!

ARCHANGELS

*A*mong the most beloved and most powerful of God's angels are the four archangels: Raphael, Michael, Gabriel, and Uriel. According to Judaic lore, each archangel has a special universal mission yet can be called on by individuals who request their assistance through prayer and invocation. Of the four, Michael most always ranks the highest and is traditionally said to "hold the keys to the Kingdom of Heaven." In fact, so invincible is Michael that in 1950 Pope Pious XXIII declared him to be the patron of police officers.

Raphael

Hebrew name: "God heals"

Mission: guardian of creative talents and universal healer

Symbol: sharp sword

Colors: pale blue and soft green

Direction: north

Season: spring

Michael

Hebrew name: "He who is like God"

Mission: prince of heavenly hosts and champion against adversity

Symbols: armor, shield, and weapon

Colors: deep green, vivid blue, rose, and gold

Direction: east

Season: summer

Gabriel

Hebrew name: "Strength of God"

Mission: angel of revelation, deliverer of good news and mercy

Symbols: trumpet; carries lily, olive branch, or torch

Colors: tans, browns, and dark green

Direction: west

Season: winter

Uriel

Hebrew name: "Fire of God"

Mission: angel of retribution and muse of artists and writers

Symbol: fiery sword

Colors: bright orange and reds

Direction: south

Season: fall

ANGEL POTPOURRI

Angel Legends

~ In ancient Rome it was customary among devoted families to thank the *Lar*, the guardian of the house, before sitting down to eat. Sometimes a special place setting was put at the table to honor this protecting angel.

~ In past centuries, when French farmers traveled by themselves on the highways, they would greet other lone travelers with "Good day to you and your companion," referring to the other's unseen but heartily acknowledged guardian angel. Even today, whenever there's a lull in a conversation the French say *"une ange passe,"* meaning that an angel has just passed over and silenced everyone's tongue.

~ Among Armenians, an old belief claims that a baby smiles because an angel is tickling the baby's feet as it tries to cut the little one's toenails.

~ In Malaysia, freckles are called "angel kisses."

~ According to one mystical Jewish story, each person lives his or her whole life in the company of two angels. The one on the person's right inspires him or her to act justly and records good deeds, and the one on the person's left nudges him or her toward evil.

Angel Accessories

Halo: holy shining light surrounding the head

Diadem: crown symbolizing royal authority

Aureola: auras of light around the body

Wings: speed and levity

Trumpet: voice of God; able to knock down walls

Lily: purity

Palm branch: victory

Angels and Fragrances

Angels sometimes trail clouds of fragrance in their wake. Those who have experienced angel sightings have often commented on the faint trace of jasmine and rose in the air. The appearance of divine masters are sometimes marked by a faint aroma of incense or rose. These are other scents associated with celestial visitations:

Pine: healing angels

Sandalwood: muses

Honeysuckle: messengers

Gardenias: heavenly response to worries about money

Hyacinth: soulful inspiration

Lilac: blessings of happiness

Angelic Last Thoughts

Angels may be vast in number—ever-present and eternal—but the fact remains that though many people believe in them, very few ever get to see them.

If you really want to see an angel, don't look for one outside; they reside within, and so long as human beings seek their own totality and wholeness, the angelic species cannot be endangered.

—*Malcolm Godwin*

The angels keep their ancient places;
Turn but a stone, and start a wing!
'Tis ye, 'tis your estranged faces,
That miss the many-splendored thing.

—*Francis Thompson*

When enough people believe (in angels), when the energy of the angels is moving through enough people, the earth will be transformed to heaven. It will happen in a twinkling.

—*Jane Howard*

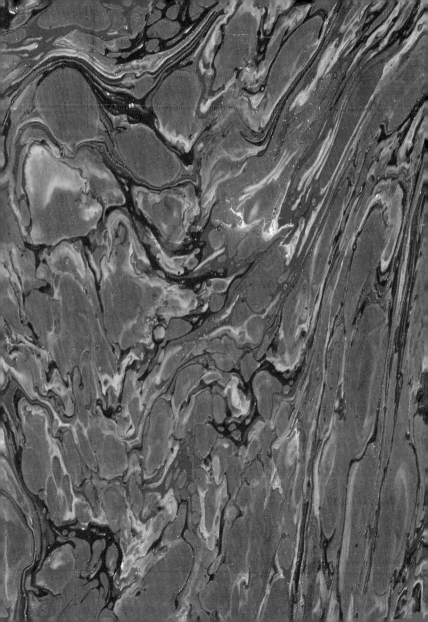